GW00499001

THE BOY KRISHNA

The Author's other works include

Krishnamurti: The Years of Awakening

Krishnamurti: The Years of Fulfilment

Krishnamurti: The Open Door

The Life and Death of Krishnamurti

To Be Young: An Autobiography

THE BOY KRISHNA

Mary Lutyens

Krishnamurti Foundation Trust Ltd.

First published in Great Britain 1995 by

Krishnamurti Foundation Trust Ltd.
Brockwood Park, Bramdean,
Hampshire SO24 0LQ, England.

For further information please write to this address.

Photograph © Krishnamurti Foundation Trust Ltd.,
England

ISBN 0 900506 13 X

Printed in Greece by Kastaniotis Editions, Athens

Typeset at Brockwood Park Krishnamurti
Educational Centre, Bramdean, Hampshire.

The account of Krishnamurti's childhood by his father, Jiddu Narianiah, is in the Adyar archives and was first published in my *Krishnamurti: The Years of Awakening* (Murray, 1975, now only available in an American paperback edition, Avon, 1984). I made an unaccountable mistake in that book in stating that Krishnamurti was born in the *puja* room of his father's house in Madanapalle, a mistake unfortunately copied in my *Life and Death of Krishnamurti* (Murray, 1990) and in Pupul Jayakar's *Krishnamurti* (Harper & Row, 1986).

Krishna age about 6

THE BOY KRISHNA

Jiddu Krishnamurti was born on Saturday, May 11, 1985 at Madanapalle, a small hill town in south India, slightly north-west of Madras. His father, Jiddu Narianiah (sometimes spelt Narayaniah), had married a second cousin, Sanjeevamma, who bore him ten children of whom Krishna was the eighth and of whom only five had survived by 1907. The family were Telegu-speaking Hindus, belonging to the highest caste, the Brahmins, and strict vegetarians. The name, which could be spelt Geddu, Giddu, Jeddu or Jiddu (it is not invariable to put the family name before the given name) was said to have been taken from the village from which the family originated, though no such village has been traced.

Krishna's paternal great-grandfather, an eminent Sanskrit scholar, and a very pious man, had held a high position in the Judicial Department of the East India Company; his grandfather, also an erudite man, had been a civil servant, while his father, after graduating from Madras University, had become an official in the Revenue Department of the British administration, rising at the end of his career to a position of *tahsildar* (rent collector) and District

Magistrate at a salary of Rs 224 a month (about £4 a week), so the family were comfortably off by Indian standards.

The family, which adhered rigidly to the Hindu caste system, lived in a small two-storeyed house in Madanapalle with an open drain running in an alley beside it carrying all the water used for household purposes. Fresh water for drinking was brought daily by the water-carriers from a nearby well and emptied into great pottery jars standing in the central courtyard where the washing hung and some of the cooking was done. The sewage was emptied by the sweepers, the 'untouchables', who belonged to no caste at all, or by the Christians who were equally despised. The sweepers were not allowed into the house except to collect sewage and, in a Brahmin household, no food could be prepared or cooked by a non-Brahmin. There was nothing, however, to prevent a poor Brahmin from doing domestic work for a richer Brahmin. The castes did not intermarry and no one could change caste except in another incarnation when, by good deeds, he had earned the right to move up the scale: this was the law of Karma.

Europeans were on a par with untouchables. Sanjeevamma would throw the food away if so much as the shadow of an Englishman fell on it, and if an Englishman entered the house the rooms were afterwards scoured and the children put into clean clothes. Narianiah could not be so particular since he had to mix with white men and even ask them on to his veranda, in the course of his employment.

Sanjeevamma had a strong premonition that this eighth child of hers was to be in some way remarkable. Narianiah himself gives an account of the birth:

It was in a small lane that we lived, at Madanapalle, in a house with an upper storey. I came to this town about the end of 1894. As an itinerary officer in Government service I had often occasion to be away on duty and returned home after one such absence, on the evening of May 11, 1895, towards sundown. I found my wife happy and cheerful, though expecting her confinement very shortly. She told me that it might happen that day, and I then asked her if she would prefer to be upstairs or downstairs. She replied that she had already selected a room on the lower storey, and had prepared it. Then I asked her if she felt well enough to sing to me; she had a very beautiful melodious voice, and liked very much to sing. She said, "Yes, but let me go upstairs". Then, reclining on an easy chair, she sang. Afterwards we had our evening meal, and retired to sleep almost in the open upstairs, because it was our hot month, May.

At about 11 o'clock my wife called me; my servants and the other children were all downstairs. She said that she was feeling ill, and asked me to bring her down. Now, as is our custom, we had a poojah [*puja*] room set apart for meditation and devotion and it was into that room she wished to go. Generally we don't enter that room at night after food, or at daybreak until we have bathed. But as she insisted upon it, I allowed her to enter the poojah room that night. She seemed very calm, and sat some time in meditation, prostrating herself in worship. Her special deity was Anjanaya, and she came out repeating that name. Then she retired to the room she had prepared, where a Brahmin lady, a relation of the family who was staying with us, assisted her. Just before the confinement, the Sudra nurse, who had been sent for from the hospital, entered, but I sat in the hall in front of the door, with my watch in my hand (the general rule with us on such occasions). After some time, the door opened, the lady friend appeared and announced: "Sirasodayam" (the head appears). It is a Sanskrit word which is always used and signifies the time from which we reckon birth. My watch recorded the hour 12.30 (midnight) Saturday 11 May 1895.[1] With the birth of the other children, my wife had suffered very much, but on this occasion it was an easy and quick birth, and all the time she muttered: "Rama, Rama, Anjanaya".

---

1 According to the calculations of Hindu astrology which reckon the day from sunrise to sunrise; thus 12.30 a.m. is still Saturday the 11th whereas by English reckoning it would have been Sunday the 12th.

Next morning the astrologer was sent for, Kumara Shrowtulu, one of the greatest astrologers in the Ceded Districts. The details of the time of birth were given to him and he retired to the *puja* room to worship and to perform the usual religious ceremonies before beginning his task. These being accomplished, he took paper and pencil and made astrological calculations. Then he told me that this boy was going to be a very great man, and continually all through the years that followed, whenever we met, he would ask me: "What of the boy Krishna?" And add: "Wait, I have told you the truth; he will be somebody very wonderful and great". Only the other day he spoke on the same subject to me.[2]

The exact date of Krishna's birth was not known until C. Jinarajadasa published his horoscope in both Sanskrit and English in the April *Theosophist* of 1932. Before that, although the year and the month did not vary, the day was variously given by Narianiah as the 4th, the 11th and the 25th—the 25th being most frequently adopted. The copies published by Jinarajadasa were copies of the original in Narianiah's writing sent to the astrologer, G. E. Sutcliffe and show

---

2 This account of Krishna's childhood was taken down in 1911 from Narianiah's dictation by Mrs Kathleen Taylor at Adyar and signed by him in the presence of two reliable witnesses. Other passages quoted from Narianiah come from the same source.

beyond all doubt that Krishna was born on Saturday, May 11, 1895 at 12.30 a.m. local time (by the Indian reckoning).

Jinarajadasa concluded that when Narianiah gave the wrong date he did not have the horoscope beside him or was too careless to consult it. Jinarajadasa also presumed that the original was written in Sanskrit on palm-leaf, as was his own. The horoscope itself is unintelligible except to astrologers but I cannot resist quoting one passage from the English translation: 'At this harmonious time (*Sattvika*), endowed with the above six *vargas*, was born the gem of a son to the great man Brahmasri Jiddu Narayaniah of the *gotra* of Harita—the full moon to the ocean of Jiddu family; endowed with everlasting day by day growing prosperity; blessed and adorned with the grace of the Lord of the Lakshmi; in the womb-ocean of his wedded wife, Srimati Sanjivamma; adorned with good luck and pure character'.[3]

For eleven days after the birth Sanjeevamma and Krishna remained together in semi-darkness while his mother fed him and rocked him in a hanging cradle made of cloth.[4] On the sixth day

---

3 I am grateful to the Theosophical Society, London, for sending me a copy of Jinarajadasa's article.
4 This is assumed by Pupul Jayakar because it was customary (*Krishnamurti*, p.17).

14

the naming ceremony was performed (presumably in semi-darkness). As the eighth child who happened to be born a boy he was called Krishnamurti in accordance with Hindu orthodoxy, in honour of Sri Krishna who had himself been an eighth son. It was a particularly appropriate name since Sanjeevamma was a worshipper of that god.

Narianiah, as well as being a Brahmin, had been for over fifteen years a member of the Theosophical Society (Theosophy embraces all religions) whose international headquarters was at Adyar, across the Adyar river just south of Madras and extending to a long sea frontage. Sanjeevamma was also interested in Theosophy, especially in Mrs Annie Besant, a prominent Theosophical leader who had done so much for Indian education. (Mrs Besant did not become President of the Society until 1907.) This is known from what Krishna himself was to relate when, at eighteen, in the summer of 1913 he was spending a holiday at Varengeville on the coast of Normandy and had been asked by his tutor to write an essay on 'Fifty Years of My Life'. He decided to make it autobiographical, adding to it every year, so that 'by the year 1945 I shall have justified the title.' All that was actually written was some 2,000 words giving a sketch of his life up to 1911. He wrote in the course of this essay:

Adyar was of special interest to me as my father used to attend the Theosophical conferences there. He also held meetings in our house for the study of Theosophy and I learnt about Adyar from my mother and from him. My mother had a *puja* room where she worshipped regularly; in the room were pictures of the Indian deities and also a photograph of Mrs Besant in Indian dress sitting cross-legged on a *chowki* or small platform on which was tiger-skin. I was generally at home while my brothers were at school because I suffered much from fever—in fact almost every day—and I often went into the *puja* room where she performed her daily ceremonies. She would then talk to me about Mrs Besant and about Karma and reincarnation and also read to me from the *Mahabharata* and *Ramayana* and from other Indian scriptures. I was only seven or eight years of age, so I could not understand much, but I think I felt much which I could not actually understand.

Sanjeevamma was to have two more children—both boys—Nityananda (Nitya), born on May 30, 1898, to whom Krishna was to become utterly devoted, and Sadanand, born in 1902, who was somewhat mentally deficient.

In November, 1896, Narianiah was transferred to Cudappah, a much larger town plagued by malaria. The following year, a very bad famine year, the two-year-old Krishna had malaria so badly that for several days he was not expected to live. Although Narianiah was transferred again in 1900 to the healthier town of Kadiri, Krishna was for many years subject to

16

periodic attacks of fever; he also suffered a good deal from nose-bleeds. Nitya too had several attacks of malaria. At Kadiri, when he was six, Krishna, like all Brahmin boys at the start of their education, went through the sacred thread ceremony, or *upanayana*. This ceremony marks their entrance into *brahmacharya*, meaning that they take on the responsibilities of Brahminhood, for every Brahmin boy is born a priest. Narianiah described this important occasion:

It is our custom to make it a family festival and friends and relations were invited to dinner. When all the people were assembled, the boy was bathed and clothed in everything new—very rich clothes are used if the parents can afford them. Krishna was brought in and placed upon my knee, while on my stretched hand I supported a silver tray strewn with grains of rice. His mother, sitting beside me, then took the index finger of the boy's right hand, and with it traced in the rice the sacred word AUM, which in its Sanskrit rendering, consists of a single letter, the letter which is, in sound, the first letter of the alphabet in Sanskrit and in all the vernaculars. Then my ring was taken from my finger, and placed between the child's finger and thumb, and my wife, holding the little hand, again traced the sacred word in Telugu characters with the ring. Then again without the ring, the same letter was traced three times. After this, *mantrams* were recited by the officiating priest, who blessed the boy, that he might be spiritually and intellectually endowed. Then, taking

Krishna with us, my wife and I drove to the Narasimhaswami temple to worship and pray for the future success of our son. From there we drove to the nearest Indian school, where Krishna was handed over to the teacher, who, in sand, performed the same ceremony of tracing the sacred word. Meanwhile, many of the friends of the schoolchildren had gathered in the room, and we distributed among them such good things as might serve as a treat to the pupils. So we started our son in his educational career according to the ancient Brahmin custom.

Krishna's little brother Nitya, just three years younger, would run after him when he went to school, longing to go too. Nitya was as sharp as Krishna was vague and dreamy; nevertheless there was a very close bond between these brothers. Krishna would often return home from school at Kadiri without a pencil, slate or book, having given them to some poorer boy. In the morning beggars would come to the house when it was the custom to pour a certain quantity of rice into each outstretched hand. Krishna's mother would send him out to distribute the rice and he would come back for more, saying that he had poured it all into the first man's bag. In the evening when Narianiah sat with his friends on the veranda, after returning from the office, beggars would come again for cooked food. This time the servants would try to drive them away but Krishna ran inside to fetch food for them, and when Sanjeevamma made a special treat of sweetmeats for the children, Krishna would take only part of his share and give the rest to his brothers; all the same Nitya would ask for more which Krishna never failed to give him.

Every evening while they were at Kadiri, Krishna and Nitya would accompany their mother to the large Narasimhaswami temple, celebrated for its sanctity. Krishna always showed a religious vein. He also surprisingly, had a mechanical turn of mind. One day, when his father was away, he took his father's clock to pieces and refused to go to school or even to eat until he had put it together again which he did satisfactorily. These two contradictory strains in his nature, as well as his generosity, persisted throughout his life.

In *Krishnamurti's Journal*, written in 1973 and published in 1982, he wrote (pp. 44-45) the only passages about his childhood that I know of apart from those in the Varengeville essay:

As a young boy he used to sit himself under a large tree near a pond in which lotuses grew; they were pink and had a strong smell. [In later years if ever he referred to himself it was in the third person.] From the shade of that spacious tree, he would watch the thin green snakes and the chameleons, the frogs and the water snakes. It was a pleasant place under the tree, with the river and the pond. There seemed to be so much space and in this the tree made its own space. Everything needs space....

The two brothers [Nitya and himself] would sit with many others in the room with the pictures [the *puja* room], there would be a chant in Sanskrit and then complete silence; it was the evening meditation. The younger brother would go to sleep and roll over and wake up only when the others got up to leave. The room was not too large and within its walls were the pictures, the images of the sacred....

To that pond would come snakes and occasionally people; it had stone steps leading down to the water.... The long, thin, green snake was there that morning; it was delicate and almost hidden among green leaves; it would be there, motionless, waiting and watching. The large head of the chameleon was showing; it lay along a branch; it changed its colours quite often.

In 1903 the family after three quick transfers were back in malaria-ridden Cudappah. (One of these quick transfers must have been to Madanapalle for there is a letter in the Adyar archives from the headmaster of the primary school there stating that Krishna had attended the school from September 1902 until the end of the year.) In 1903, at Cudappah, Krishna's eldest sister died. Narianiah recorded that his wife 'was heart-broken at our daughter's death, a girl of only twenty years, highly spiritual, who cared for nothing that the world could give her.' It was after her death that Krishna showed for the first time that he was clairvoyant. In his Varengeville essay he was to write that his mother was 'to a certain extent psychic and would often see her dead daughter':

They talked together and there was a special place in the garden to which my sister used to come. My mother always knew when my sister was there and sometimes took me with her to the place, and would ask me whether I saw my sister too. At first I laughed at the question, but she asked me to look again and then sometimes I saw my sister. Afterwards I could always see my sister. I must confess I was very much afraid, because I had seen her dead and her body burnt. I generally rushed to my mother's side and she told me there was no reason to be afraid. I was the only member of the family, except my mother, to see these visions, though all believed in them. My mother was able to see the auras of people, and I also sometimes saw them.

In December 1905, when Krishna was ten and a half and the family were still at Cudappah, a terrible blow fell on them—Sanjeevamma herself died. Krishna wrote in his Varengeville essay:

The happiest memories of my childhood centred round my dear mother who gave us all the loving care for which Indian mothers are well known. I cannot say I was particularly happy at school, for the teachers were not very kind and gave me lessons that were too hard for me. I enjoyed games as long as they were not too rough, as I had very delicate health.

My mother's death in 1905 deprived my brothers and myself of the one who loved and cared for us most, and my father was too much occupied to pay much attention to us. There was really nobody to look after us. In connection with my mother's death I may mention that I frequently saw her after she died. I remember once following my mother's form as she went upstairs. I stretched out my hand and seemed to catch hold of her dress, but she vanished as soon as she reached the top of the stairs. Until a short time ago, I used to hear my mother following me as I went to school. I remember this particularly because I heard the sound of bangles which Indian women wear on their wrist. At first I would look back half frightened, and I saw the vague form of her dress and part of her face. This happened almost always when I went out of the house.

Narianiah confirmed that Krishna saw his dead mother:

We are in the habit of putting out on a leaf, a portion of the food prepared for the household, and placing it near the spot where the deceased was lying, and we did so accordingly in the case of my wife. Between nine and ten a.m. of the third day, Krishna was going to have his bath. He went into the bathroom, and had only poured a few *lotas* of water over his head, when he came out, unclothed [though wearing a loin-cloth] and dripping wet. The house in which I lived at Cudappah was a long, narrow house, the rooms running one at the back of the other like the compartments of a train. As Krishna passed me running from the bathroom, I caught his hand and asked him what was the matter. The boy said his mother had been in the bathroom with him, and as she came out he accompanied her to see what she was going to do. I then said: "Don't you remember that your mother was carried to the burning ground?" "Yes" he replied, "I remember, but I want to see where she is going now." I let him go and followed him. He went to the third room and stopped. Here was the place where my wife's *saris* used to be stretched for drying overnight. Krishna stood intently gazing at something, and I asked him what was going on. He said, "My mother is removing her wet clothes and putting on dry ones." He then went into the next room, and sat down near the leaf on which the food was placed. I stood by him some minutes, and he said his mother was eating. By and by he arose and went towards the stairs, and still I followed him. He stopped half-way up, and said he couldn't see her any more. Then we sat down together and I questioned him on how she looked, and whether she spoke to him. He said she looked just as usual, and had not spoken to him.

After his wife's death Narianiah took a few months' leave and returned to Madanapalle for the sake of the children's health; when he resumed service again he was able to remain there until his retirement. Krishna and Nitya were both admitted on January 17, 1907, to the

23

high school at Madanapalle which they attended until January, 1909.

About two miles from their house was a lonely hill with a temple on the top and Krishna liked to go there every day after school. None of the other boys wanted to accompany him, as it was a stiff climb over stony ground, but he would often insist on taking Nitya with him. He also liked taking his friends on picnics. As his father was now a District Magistrate, a position of some importance, Krishna's brothers considered it beneath their dignity to carry the food to the picnic spot; Krishna, who had no such feelings of self-importance, would take the food from the servants and carry it himself.

At the end of 1907, at the age of fifty-two, Narianiah was obliged to retire on a pension of Rs 112 a month, half his former salary. He then wrote to Mrs Besant, who had recently become President of the Theosophical Society, to offer his 'whole-hearted and full-time service' in any capacity in exchange for free accommodation in the Theosophical compound at Adyar for himself and his sons. He told her that when in Government service he had been in charge of 800 square miles containing 150 villages and felt that he would be able to manage a fairly large estate; he also told her that he was a widower with four sons, ranging in age from fifteen to five, that his only living daughter was married and that there was no one to look after the boys.

Mrs Besant refused his offer on the grounds that there was no school nearer than three miles, that this would involve the expense of sending the children there in a pony-cart and that, anyway boys would be a disturbance in the compound. Narianiah persisted, each time receiving a refusal. Then suddenly at the end of 1908 one of the secretaries of the Society came to need an assistant and suggested Narianiah for the position. Mrs Besant at last agreed to employ him after meeting him at the Theosophical Convention in December 1908, and on January 23, 1909, he moved to Adyar with his four sons, but since there was no house available inside the compound the family were put in a dilapidated cottage just outside it. The eldest son, Sivaram, who became a doctor, joined the Presidency College in Madras while Krishna and Nitya went to the Pannaphur Subramanian High School at Mylapore, walking the three miles every day there and back. Little Sadanand was not well enough physically or mentally to go to school at all.

Lessons were conducted mostly in English of which Krishna knew very little. So stupid did he appear that the teacher would frequently send him out of the classroom on to the veranda and forget all about him until he called some other boy stupid when he would be remembered and brought in again. He was caned almost every day for not learning his lessons. Sometimes he remained forgotten on the veranda until the end of the school day when Nitya would come out and find him standing there in tears and lead him home by the hand.

The boys arrived at Adyar in shocking physical condition, undernourished, covered in mosquito bites and with lice even in their eyebrows. At first an aunt, a sister of Narianiah who had quarrelled with her husband, came to look after them but she was a slatternly woman and a very bad cook; she stayed only a short time and after she left there was no one to look after them.

The only pleasure the boys had was in going down to the beach in the evenings to paddle with the village boys and watch the swimmers from the Theosophical compound. The compound stretched down to a wide expanse of almost deserted sandy beach at a place where the wide Adyar river ran into the Bay of Bengal; this was the so-called Coromandel Coast.

Less than three weeks after Narianiah and his family had settled in their cottage, Charles Webster Leadbeater, a clairvoyant and important lecturer for the Theosophical Society, arrived at Adyar after an absence of nearly seven years during which he had been involved in a scandal in England to do with his teaching of young boys. He had resigned from the Society but after Mrs Besant became president in 1907 she worked hard to clear his name and eventually succeeded in reinstating him. He returned to live and work at Adyar as he had done before but he was never again to hold any official position in the Society. Two of his young secretaries drew his attention to Krishna and Nitya whom they had met and become interested in when they went for their evening swim. Leadbeater then went himself to the beach and was immediately struck by the beauty of Krishna's aura which, he maintained, had not a trace of selfishness in it.

But it was not until some time towards the end of April that he asked Narianiah to bring Krishna to the Octagon Bungalow where he lived, close to the Headquarters buildings. He then sat him down on the sofa beside him and put his hand on the boy's head. In the meantime he had been watching him closely, particularly during Nitya's sacred thread ceremony which took place unprecedentedly late—he was nearly eleven—no doubt because of the general neglect of the boys after their mother's death.

Krishna was to write in his Varengeville essay:

When I first went over to his [Leadbeater's] room I was much afraid, for most Indian boys are afraid of Europeans. I do not know why it is that such fear is created, but apart from the difference in colour which is no doubt one of the causes, there was when I was a boy, much political agitation and our imaginations were much stirred by the gossip about us. I must also confess that the Europeans in India are by no means generally kind to us and I used to see many acts of cruelty which made me still more bitter. It was a surprise to us, therefore, to find how different was the Englishman who was also a Theosophist.

This is the end of Krishna's Indian boyhood.

Some more details of Krishna's childhood have come to light within recent years from a very strange source. As everyone who has read his story will know, he underwent an intense three-day spiritual experience in the summer of 1922 which completely changed his life. At the time he was living alone with Nitya in the Ojai Valley, California, in a cottage lent to him by an American Theosophist, Mrs Mary Gray, close to her own house. Nitya had had a recurrence of the tuberculosis from which he had suffered on and off from the spring of 1921 and the brothers had stopped in California on the way from Sydney to Switzerland, having been advised that the Ojai Valley had just as good a climate as Switzerland for this disease.

They had arrived at Ojai on July 6, 1922, and were to find it a paradise. Not long afterwards an American girl of nineteen, Rosalind Williams, who was staying with Mrs Gray, met them and made immediate friends with them. She had a particularly good influence on Nitya who did what she told him whereas he would become very irritable when Krishna tried to make him rest. Rosalind, with her mother's consent, stayed on with Mrs Gray and went every day to the cottage as Nitya's unofficial nurse.

Rosalind was with the brothers when Krishna's experience took place between August 17th and 20th[5], as was also Mr A P Warrington, General Secretary of the Theosophical society in America, who had first recommended the Ojai Valley to them and who had another cottage in the Valley close by.

It was two weeks after this, on September 3rd, that there started for Krishna what Nitya was to call the 'process'. This was appalling pain in different parts of the body but mostly in his head and spine which came on regularly at 6.30 every evening and lasted for an hour or so. (There was very little pain with the three day experience.) But little if any of Krishna's consciousness was there during these sessions and it was what Nitya called 'the physical elemental' that was left to bear the pain—that is, the part of the body that controls its instinctive and purely physical actions when the higher consciousness is withdrawn. The physical elemental was said to be at a low stage of evolution and needed constant guidance.

Again it was Nitya, Rosalind and Mr Warrington who were present every evening

---

5 An account of this was first published in *Krishnamurti: The Years of Awakening*.

during the 'process', but now Krishna mistook Rosalind for his mother. This nightly occurrence, with variations, went on until the end of December.

Throughout these weeks Nitya, whose life had also been completely changed since the three-day experience in August, kept notes each day of Krishna's conditions and when the 'process' eventually stopped, put his notes together 'so as to keep a coherent record' of all that had happened to send to Mrs Besant and Leadbeater. This record runs to forty-seven quarto pages of typescript. Since Nitya could not type someone must have typed it for him, presumably Rosalind's elder Theosophical sister, but it is signed in Nitya's writing: 'Nitya Feb. 11. 23'.

Both Krishna and Nitya believed that the 'process' was essential for the preparation of Krishna's body for the acceptance of the Lord Maitreya, the World Teacher, and must on no account be stopped or interrupted. Krishna remembered nothing of what happened while he was unconscious but, when the torturing process was over and he had 'come back', he would sit with the others drinking milk (he had no evening meal all this time) and want to know what had happened while he was 'away'. Nevertheless, although he had no memory of the atrocious pain his body had undergone, the body itself suffered from it and Krishna became more and more weary and emaciated as the days went by. Nitya too suffered physically from having to watch such pain and Rosalind began to feel the strain.

On the evening of October 6th a new phenomenon took place at the end of the regular session of suffering. As usual Krishna had some difficulty in regaining consciousness. Nitya recorded:

Little by little his energy began to return and later he began to talk in a faint whisper. Gradually his voice became stronger and when we could make out what he was saying we realized, with amazement, that it was not the Krishna that we knew who was talking, but Krishna the child, the small boy of four, or perhaps less. He was talking in good English, but like a child, simply, and he was talking of the early days of his childhood, living over again early scenes. He saw three distinct scenes of his early life and as he talked of them we could almost see them ourselves, so vivid were his feelings and expressions. The first scene was of his mother giving birth to a child. This was a terrible shock to him and with every spasm of agony that he saw, he moaned and shrieked as she must have done. Again and again he would say "O poor mother, poor mother, you are brave, mother." Then he was silent for a little and now the scene changed. We were both lying ill with malaria, Krishna and I. Krishna, as he saw us, was very much affected by the sight of the poor thin bodies, sick with the shivering malaria, the great big tummies swollen with eating so much rice. The last scene was the death of his mother. He could not understand what was happening; he thought she was ill and when he saw the doctor giving her medicine, he became very indignant. He began begging his mother "Don't take it mother, don't take it, it is some beastly stuff and it won't do you any good, please don't take it, the doctor does not know anything, he is a dirty man, please don't take it mother." And when eventually she did take it, he gave her up. He said "Mother they are giving you awful food, they're killing you mother." A little later, in a tone of horror he said, "Why are you so still mother, what's happened, and why does father cover his face with his *dhoti*, mother, answer me mother", and all the time he would expect Rosalind to answer him; but to explain death to him was too great a task so we gently woke him up after he ceased talking of what he saw. But till he woke up, he was like a child of four, his voice was even that of a child, and he spoke of himself as a child.

The next night at the end of the process he again became a small child and talked of his childhood:

He must have loathed his school life, for he was always asking "Mother I need not go to school today need I? I'm awfully ill mother" he would say, and when he thought she realized this to be an excuse he would say, "Mother let me stay with you, I'll do anything you want, I'll take castor oil, if you like, but let me stay with you." His dislike of school was as great as his love of the temples. When he could escape the

32

former he would beg to be taken to the temple. He said to his mother suddenly, "Mother I've got lots of small biscuits in my pocket, they're awfully good", and Rosalind said she was glad he liked them; this surprised him greatly. "Mother, you know you hid the box of biscuits from us, well, I stole these from that box, I've been doing it for a long, long time". And Rosalind would become carefully grave and if she did not restrain her laughter, as sometimes it happened to both of us, he became very hurt and he would say "Mother you are always laughing at me, why do you laugh at me?" So Rosalind in a serious voice asked him if he thought it was nice to steal, besides which, she said, "Why do you tell me this now, if you've been doing it for a long time?" His answer nearly broke her gravity. "You see mother the box is nearly finished and you've suspected me for a long time, so I thought I'd better tell you". Still later after talking a great deal about snakes, puppies and beggars he talked of going into the shrine room where he saw a picture of a lady sitting cross-legged on a deerskin. I had a vague memory that it might be a picture of A.B. [Annie Besant] and I suggested this. Krishna did not know her name. "Who is that?" he asked, "She looks like someone I know, only she does not look like that, she's quite different." Then gradually he woke up. Even after he was awake, if he was too near Rosalind and she touched him, he would be off, and he would begin talking of mother and his voice would change. The rapidity with which he could leave his body was extraordinary.

I now string together all Nitya recorded about Krishna's childhood, omitting the much longer passages describing his suffering:

The effort of coming back into his body made him shudder and tremble for a long time, and this shuddering would so exhaust him that he would lie still, unable to speak or make any movement. Presently, when he began to speak, it was the child speaking and after talking of his childhood for about thirty minutes he woke up. This became the regular order of events after the night of 5th [of October]. First the meditation till six; when he came from his meditation Rosalind would be with him for about ten minutes, then would come the great pain and the sobbing and the period when Krishna was out of his body and only the elemental would be speaking.[6] Then towards 7.30 Rosalind would go into the room, and the shuddering and the contortions would begin; towards eight o'clock he would become the child, and he would talk until he wished to

6 Messages and instructions would be relayed in Krishna's own adult voice through 'the physical elemental' from unknown, unseen beings who were apparently looking after him and making sure that his body was not strained beyond endurance. Krishna himself was also heard by Nitya and Rosalind talking to these beings.

wake up, when he would say, "Mother wake me up, Nitya must go to bed." Sometimes he would talk for an hour of his childhood, sometimes even longer; Krishna is not naturally talkative, but when he became a child, his flow of words is extraordinary. We, of course, were very interested in what he had to say, so the talking would go on sometimes till ten o'clock. We learned a good deal about Krishna's character as a child, and his interests in the days of his childhood.... On the 13th there was very little pain. He groaned a little at first, then there was absolute silence till 7.30, and Rosalind and I sat outside and waited for him to waken. When he called out for his mother she went in and straightaway he began talking to her as a child having a great deal to tell her and full of innumerable questions as a child would be.... That night [the 14th], when he became a child, we learnt that he used to see fairies and that there was one particular fairy who used to be a special friend, and who came often to play with him. The fairy was apparently very beautiful in reality and had beautiful clothes, but in consideration for Krishna, when he came to play with him he made himself ugly, 'just like me' as Krishna put it. He talked a great deal of this fairy and of the games they used to have together. Krishna must have been an awfully nice child. The 15th, 16th and 17th were peaceful nights, with practically no pain; he talked of going far away where it was very lonely. As the pain decreased, he became a child for longer and longer periods. There was a certain consecutiveness in this living over of his childhood. He talked one night of a journey in a bullock cart, and the next night he talked of this journey of three or four days being finished. Whether this continuity was progressive or retrogressive I cannot tell. He talked of me as a small child who could hardly walk, and who had to be taken care of and with this was mixed up the idea of my present illness and need for rest.... The night of the 20th saw the definite end of the sufferings.... Krishna was told to rest the next few nights. We had thought of going to Hollywood on the 26th and he was told that this would be all right only he should take a complete rest first. So on the 21st, 22nd, 23rd, 24th and 25th, Krishna went to bed in the evening at 6.30 immediately after his meditation. Rosalind would sit by him and for two hours and more Krishna became a little child, maintaining a steady flow of conversation the whole time. Occasionally, Rosalind would say "Now Krishna go to sleep for a little while;" he would keep quiet for a very few minutes, then he would say, "Let me talk now, mother, will you? You need not listen to me if you don't want to, but I like to talk". And he would start again. He told us once that his friend the fairy was a great talker, and we asked him in fun, who talked the most, the fairy or himself. He said he would ask the fairy and tell us the day after. The next night we had forgotten our question but he remembered. He said "You know mother, the fairy talks more than I do, I listen all the time." And so during the next five days we learnt a great deal of the child Krishna. One curious fact we noticed was this. The child Krishna had no remembrance of what happened during the day. He would say, "Mother why do you go away during the day? You never talk to me during the day." And he would reproach her bitterly for leaving him like that.

They were in Hollywood on the 26th and until November 9th nothing happened in the evenings. But on the 10th evening he again became unconscious, and was transformed into the child. He asked Rosalind to tell Krishna that this would happen every other night. Until December 5th he became a child every other night; it ceased because Rosalind was unable to be with him for she had to have a minor operation on her nose. On December 9th they returned to Ojai and until January 7 there was no return of this evening process. On the 7th and 8th he became a child for two hours in the evening. This was the last occurrence.

Although Krishna, the small boy talking in his childish voice, was to appear in other sessions, at different times and in different places, mistaking two other girls for his mother, he was never again to 'bring through' any recollections of his childhood. He would address these girls as 'Amma', which is what he would have called his real mother. Surprisingly, in this first session, as described by Nitya, he called Rosalind 'Mother', but this may have been a translation by Nitya.

Krishna was often asked in later life what he thought would have happened to him if he had not been 'discovered' by Leadbeater. He would unhesitatingly reply, 'I would have died'. There is only one published reference by him to the time after his discovery. This appears in his *Journal* of 1973 (p. 26):

He [Krishna himself] was standing there with no one around, alone, unattached and far away. He was fourteen or less [actually fifteen]. And all the fuss and sudden importance given to him was around him. He was the centre of respect and devotion and in the years to come he would be the head of organisations and great properties. All that and the dissolution of them still lay ahead. Standing there alone, lost and strangely aloof, was his first and lasting remembrance of those days and events.